MASTERING DIGITAL WELLBEING AMONG SCHOOL KIDS

DR DHEERAJ MEHROTRA

Contents

Preface

As the digital world evolves rapidly, technology has become indispensable to our everyday lives, particularly for youngsters. The use of digital gadgets is pervasive in a child's environment, including everything from social interactions to educational aids. Many advantages may be gained from technology, yet it also brings obstacles that can affect the physical, emotional, and mental well-being of children. By providing teachers, parents, and other caregivers with the information and resources they need to promote digital wellness among school-aged children, the purpose of this book is to empower them.

I can ensure that children have a healthy and balanced relationship with technology by first gaining knowledge of the complexities of digital well-being and then implementing beneficial solutions.

www.authordheerajmehrotra.com

CHAPTER ONE

Introduction to Digital Wellbeing

Recognizing the Importance of Digital Health

When discussing our physical, emotional, and mental health, we refer to technology's impact on our digital well-being. The concept involves the equilibrium between using digital devices and preserving a healthy way of life. This equilibrium is of the utmost importance when it comes to children who are still in the formative stages of their development. Their wellness can be badly impacted by excessive screen time, the pressures of social media, and the possibility of being bullied online.

On the other hand, when utilized with awareness, technology has the potential to boost learning, develop creativity, and strengthen social ties.

• 3 •

Understanding the Digital Well-being of Kids:

How technology shapes the digital well-being of school-going children is a complicated and diverse problem deserving of careful thought. Knowing the

possible advantages and hazards of using digital devices and online platforms is essential as they become increasingly ingrained in children's lives—at home and school.

Digital well-being for children is maintaining a healthy lifestyle that fosters physical, emotional, and mental growth while using technology for social and educational objectives. This balance is vital during the formative years when children form habits and behaviours that can last into adulthood.

One of the main worries about kids' digital welfare is too much screen time. Extended usage of digital gadgets might result in a sedentary lifestyle, aggravating physical health problems, including obesity, bad posture, and eye strain. The American Academy of Pediatrics advises children to limit their screen time, with particular recommendations depending on age groups. Enforcing these restrictions, however, can be difficult, mainly when digital devices are utilized for leisure and learning.

Furthermore, too much screen time might disrupt essential activities such as face-to-face social contact, physical activity, and sleep. Sleep disturbance can negatively affect a child's general well-being, affecting cognitive ability, emotional control, and academic achievement. Children's natural sleep-wake cycle may be disrupted, and melatonin generation suppressed by blue light emitted by screens makes falling asleep more difficult.

Social media poses still another major threat to

children's digital welfare. These sites expose children to different hazards even though they can help them connect and communicate. Maintaining a deliberate online presence can cause anxiety, low self-esteem, and a false view of reality. Children could develop poor body image and feelings of inadequacy by comparing themselves to classmates or unrealistic ideals pushed on social media.

One very troubling feature of children's internet encounters is cyberbullying. Digital platforms' anonymity and remoteness can empower bullies, therefore enabling more severe and ongoing kinds of abuse. Cyberbullying victims could suffer from anxiety, depression, and, in severe situations, suicidal thoughts. Given the ubiquitous character of internet communication, youngsters could feel helpless in avoiding bullying even in their homes.

Privacy and data security are also essential factors in children's digital well-being. Many young people lack the knowledge and experience to properly negotiate online privacy settings or grasp the possible long-term effects of posting personal information online. Thus, they may be susceptible to data leaks, identity theft, or malicious actor exploitation.

Notwithstanding these obstacles, it's crucial to understand that, when utilized deliberately, technology can have significant positive effects on kids' growth and welfare. Digital tools can improve educational opportunities by offering interactive and exciting instructional materials that fit various learning environments. Personalized learning *experiences made possible by educational applications and platforms let kids advance at their speed and concentrate on areas needing extra help.*

Additionally, it encourages creativity and self-expression through technology. Children now have new resources to pursue their creative hobbies, from digital art tools, music creation software, and video editing platforms. Programs in robotics and coding can expose kids to STEM disciplines in exciting ways and maybe inspire lifetime interests in these topics.

Moreover, internet channels can help children stay in touch with friends and relatives who might live far away, strengthening social ties. These digital contacts become even more critical for children's social and emotional well-being during periods of social separation, including the current worldwide epidemic.

Positive digital well-being for school-going children requires a diverse strategy combining parents, teachers, and technology creators. Setting reasonable limits and modelling good technological use depend much on parents. Establishing tech-free zones or periods in the house, pushing outside activities and in-person meetings, and candidly sharing internet experiences with their kids could all help.

By including digital literacy in their courses, teachers may teach their students how to assess online material critically, guard their privacy, and use technology responsibly. Schools can also enforce rules for acceptable online behaviour or device-free intervals during the day, encouraging balanced technology use.

Technology creators are responsible for designing products and platforms considering children's well-being. This can entail building solid parental controls, using tools that inspire screen-time breaks, or inventing algorithms that prioritize positive, age-appropriate content.

Policymakers also have a responsibility to protect children's digital well-being. This might include financing digital literacy initiatives, rules on data collection and targeted advertising to minors, or orders for technology companies to prioritise kid safety in their product designs.

The ultimate aim is to encourage a good relationship with digital tools rather than eradicate them from youngsters' lives. Children should be taught to be thoughtful consumers of technology, allowing them to see its advantages and negatives. By arming them with the tools to negotiate the digital world safely and ethically, we can help guarantee that technology improves rather than compromises children's general well-being.

We must keep researching and adjusting our strategies for children's digital well-being as we enter an increasingly digital environment. This could entail inventing new measures for evaluating digital health, building more complex tools for controlling online experiences, and learning about new technologies and how they might affect child development.

Ultimately, the digital well-being of school-going children is a significant concern that calls for continuous attention and work from all involved parties. Children will flourish in the digital age if we can strike a balance between the advantages of technology and the maintenance of physical, emotional, and mental health. This will assist in developing the skills and resilience children need for a promising, prosperous future.

Finding a Balance Is Very Important

Establishing the appropriate balance is necessary to achieve digital well-being. It is not about doing away with technology; instead, it is about incorporating it to encourage healthy living. Limit children's time spent in front of screens, encourage them to engage in physical activities, communicate with one another in person, and teach them how to use technology responsibly.

Here are essential ideas to keep in mind for children reaching digital well-being:

1. The aim is to combine technology to foster general health and development rather than eradicate it.

2. Establish and enforce realistic limitations for gadget use according to the child's age and need.

3. To offset inactive screen time, advocate regular exercise and outdoor play.

4. Give top priority to face-to-face contacts. Provide chances for direct social interaction to hone vital people skills.

5. Children should be taught responsible technology use, including internet safety, privacy, and ethical behaviour in digital environments.

6. Model good practices: Adults should show in their own lives balanced usage of technology.

7. Create tech-free zones in the house where devices are off-limits, like during meals or before bed.

8. Encourage a spectrum of interests and pastimes outside of digital consumption.

9. Children should be taught to assess internet material and spot possible hazards or false information.

10. Emphasize using digital tools for learning, creativity, and meaningful communication rather than passive consumption in your use of technology.

11. Track material: Know what kids view online and use sensible parent limits.

12. Emphasize the need to rest eyes and minds by employing digital breaks from screens routinely.

13. Encourage excellent sleeping hygiene: Reduce device use before bed to guarantee quality sleep.

14. Talk about internet encounters. Keep lines of open contact regarding children's digital lives and any worries they might have.

15. As children develop and their needs vary, routinely review and modify technology policies.

16. Considering these factors, parents and teachers can help children develop a positive connection with technology that improves rather than compromises their general well-being.

CHAPTER TWO

Common Digital Challenges for School Kids

Time Management for Screen Time

Time management is one of the most severe issues that has to be addressed. Children frequently spend extended periods using digital devices, which can result in a variety of health issues, including eye strain, sleep difficulties, and lifestyles that are considered to be sedentary. Limiting the time spent in front of a screen and encouraging regular breaks are two ways to lessen these impacts. Practical time management skills are essential for children's overall health and development, especially when

using electronic devices. Excessive screen time, caused by digital gadgets' ubiquitous and appealing nature, can severely affect children's physical, mental, and general development.

Eye strain, often known as computer vision syndrome or digital eye strain, is a significant issue. Symptoms, including headaches, dry eyes, and blurred vision, can be brought on by staring at computer screens for lengthy periods. Another possible cause of insomnia caused by these devices is the blue light they emit, which might disrupt the body's natural circadian rhythms. The hormone melatonin regulates sleep, and when kids use electronics late at night, it might delay its release. This makes it harder for them to fall asleep and may even affect the quality of their sleep.

Additionally, a sedentary lifestyle is frequently associated with excessive screen usage. Kids who sit in front of screens for long periods are less likely to play outside and may be at increased risk for obesity and its complications. This inactivity might also affect their fitness levels and motor skills development.

Creating techniques to regulate and limit screen time is critical to solve these difficulties. Here are a few methods that work:

Limit screen time according to age-appropriate norms. The American Academy of Pediatrics has some suggestions to get things rolling.

1. Opt for parental control features: Restricting device or app use is a great feature for younger children.

2. Promote taking frequent breaks: The 20-20-20 rule states that you should look at something 20 feet away for 20 seconds every 20 minutes. This can reduce eye strain.

3. Establish unplugged areas and periods: To encourage other hobbies and face-to-face encounters, set off specific spaces (like bedrooms) or times (like meals) where devices are not allowed.

4. Encourage other pursuits: Prompt them to engage in activities away from screens, such as playing physically, reading, and being creative.

5. Make balanced use of technology a habit by setting a good example as parents and caregivers.

6. For better sleep hygiene, institute a digital curfew: switch off all electronic devices at a particular hour every night.

7. Make screen time a reward instead of a right; this will teach kids to see it as a privilege, not a right, and could lead to less usage overall.

8. Make people aware of the effects: Help kids realize the importance of limiting their screen usage for their health and happiness.

9. Provide alerts before screen time is up and have fun things to do when you switch it off to help with transitions.

10. Remember that different screen time forms have other effects.

There may be a difference between the effects of passively consuming entertainment and those of educational content or creative digital activities. Consequently, it's not enough to limit overall screen time; one must also ensure that digital device use is productive and well-balanced.

A Priority:

When you try to implement these tactics consistently, you may encounter pushback at first. Nonetheless, kids may learn to use their phones

and other digital devices responsibly with time and effort. Teaching children how to use technology in a balanced way is essential to ensure that technology does not negatively affect their health and development.
We can promote a balanced approach to digital device usage and aid youngsters with time management so that technology contributes to their well-being and growth instead of hindering them.

Mental Health and the Role of Social Media

Two sides of the same coin can be found on social media. Although it provides opportunities for sociability and self-expression, it can also result in problems such as low self-esteem, anxiety, and sadness of the individual. The importance of teaching youngsters about the benefits and drawbacks of social media and encouraging them to use it mindfully cannot be overstated.

Online safety and the issue of cyberbullying

It is a big problem that can have severe emotional and psychological repercussions, and cyberbullying is one of those problems. To effectively tackle this issue, it is essential to educate children about the importance of online safety, how to identify and report instances of cyberbullying and cultivate a supportive environment. Here are critical points on addressing cyberbullying and its emotional and psychological impacts on children:

• Cyberbullying is a serious issue with potentially severe consequences for children's mental health and well-being.

• Education is crucial:
- Teach children about online safety and responsible digital citizenship
- Help them identify different forms of cyberbullying
- Instruct on how to report incidents to trusted adults or platform moderators

• Create a supportive environment:
- Encourage open communication about online experiences
- Assure children it's not their fault if they're bullied
- Emphasize the importance of speaking up and seeking help

- *Develop coping strategies:*
- *Teach children not to engage with or retaliate against bullies*
- *Show how to block or mute abusive users*
- *Encourage preserving evidence of bullying incidents*

- *Foster empathy and kindness online:*
- *Discuss the impact of words and actions in digital spaces*
- *Encourage positive online interactions*

- *Implement school policies:*
- *Establish clear anti-cyberbullying guidelines*
- *Provide resources for reporting and addressing incidents*

- *Involve parents and guardians:*
- *Educate them about cyberbullying risks and signs*
- *Encourage monitoring of children's online activities*

- *Promote digital literacy:*
- *Teach critical thinking skills for navigating online content*
- *Help children understand the permanence of digital actions*

- *Provide access to support services:*
- *Ensure children know about helplines or*

counselling resources
- Offer mental health support for those affected by cyberbullying

CHAPTER THREE

Physical Health in the Digital Age

Reducing the Effects of Digital Eye Strain

Children who spend a significant amount of time in front of screens are more likely to experience some digital eye strain, often called computer vision syndrome. Headaches, blurred vision, and dry eyes are some of the symptoms that may exist. It may be possible to prevent these symptoms by encouraging people to follow the 20-20-20 rule, which is taking a 20-second break every 20 minutes to look at something 20 feet away.

Digital eye strain is common for children who spend extensive time using screens. Symptoms like headaches, blurred vision, and dry eyes can significantly impact a child's comfort and ability to focus. The 20-20-20 rule is an effective strategy to combat these problems:

1.

Every 20 minutes

2.

Take a 20-second break

3.

Look at something 20 feet away

This simple practice helps reduce eye fatigue by allowing the eyes to refocus and relax. It also encourages children to disconnect from their screens, briefly promoting better digital habits. Parents and educators should actively encourage and remind children to follow this rule, potentially using timer apps or visual cues to make it a routine part of screen time.

Promoting a Fit and Proper Posture

Poor posture can cause problems with the musculoskeletal system. Good posture can be maintained by teaching children to sit correctly and use ergonomically designed furniture. In addition, regular physical exercise is an essential factor in preventing posture-related problems. Poor posture during screen use is a significant concern for children's musculoskeletal health.

Here are key points to address this issue:

• *Importance of proper posture:*

  • *Prevents strain on muscles, joints, and spine*

  • *Reduces risk of long-term musculoskeletal problems*

  • *Improves overall comfort and focus*

• *Teaching correct sitting posture:*

  • *Feet flat on the floor*

  • *Knees at or slightly below hip level*

  • *Back straight and supported*

  • *Shoulders relaxed*

  •

Screen at eye level or slightly below

- *Ergonomic furniture:*

  - *Adjustable chairs and desks to accommodate growth*

  - *Supportive seating that encourages proper spine alignment*

  - *Footrests, if needed, to maintain proper leg position*

- *Regular physical exercise:*

  - *Strengthens core muscles, supporting good posture*

  - *Improves flexibility and range of motion*

  - *Counters the effects of prolonged sitting*

- *Encourage movement breaks:*

- *Regular intervals to stand, stretch, and walk around*

- *Incorporate active sitting (e.g., stability balls) when appropriate*

- *Education and awareness:*

- Teach children about the importance of good posture
- Demonstrate proper techniques for device use

- *Parental and educator involvement:*

- *Monitor and correct posture regularly*

- *Lead by example with good posture habits*

- *Balanced lifestyle:*

- *Limit extended periods of screen time*

- *Promote a mix of seated and standing activities*

By implementing these strategies, we can help children develop good posture habits, reduce the risk of musculoskeletal issues, and promote overall physical well-being in the digital age.

The encouragement of physical activity

Maintaining a healthy balance between time spent in front of screens and moving about is essential for general wellness. To combat the passive nature of screen time, it is possible to encourage activities such as soccer, playing outside, and other forms of physical activity.

Here are key points for maintaining a healthy balance between screen time and physical activity:

Importance of balance:

- *Essential for overall physical and mental health*

- *Counteracts sedentary behaviour associated with screen use*

Benefits of physical activity:

- *Improves cardiovascular health*

- *Strengthens muscles and bones*

- *Enhances coordination and motor skills*

- *Boosts mood and reduces stress*

- *Aids in maintaining a healthy weight*

Encouraging outdoor activities:

- *Promotes vitamin D synthesis*

- *It provides a change of scenery and fresh air*

- *Offers varied terrain for motor skill development*

Team sports like soccer:

- *Develops social skills and teamwork*

- *Teaches strategy and decision-making*

- *Provides structured physical activity*

Other physical activities to promote:

- *Cycling*

- *Swimming*

- *Dance*

- *Martial arts*

- *Gymnastics*

- *Playground games*

Integrating movement with screen time:

- *Active video games that require physical movement*

- *Screen breaks for quick exercises or stretches*

Setting a positive example:

-

Parents and educators should model active lifestyles

Creating a supportive environment:

- *Providing access to sports equipment*

- *Identifying safe spaces for outdoor play*

Establishing routines:

- *Scheduling regular times for physical activity*

- *Limiting screen time, especially before bedtime*

Making physical activity fun:

- *Choosing activities that align with the child's interests*

-

Incorporating elements of play and creativity

Gradual increase in activity:

- *Starting with small, achievable goals*

- *Slowly building up the duration and intensity of physical activity*

Monitoring progress:

- *Tracking improvements in fitness and well-being*

- *Celebrating achievements to maintain motivation*

CHAPTER FOUR

Mental Health and Digital Spaces

Understanding the Signs of Addiction to Digital Media

Addiction to digital media can express itself in some ways, including an inability to limit screen time, withdrawal symptoms when not using gadgets, and a neglect of activities that take place offline. To keep one's mental health in good standing, it is vital to recognize these indicators early and address them proactively.

Methods for Handling Stress and Anxiety

The constant flow of information and the need to compare oneself to others are two factors that might contribute to feelings of worry and stress brought on by the digital world. Teaching children stress management strategies, such as mindfulness and relaxation exercises, can assist them in coping with the pressures associated with digital technology. Here are critical points on managing stress and anxiety caused by the digital world:

- *Recognize digital stressors:*
- *Information overload*
- *Social comparison on social media*
- *Fear of missing out (FOMO)*
- *Pressure to be constantly available*

- *Teach mindfulness techniques:*
- *Focused breathing exercises*
- *Body scan meditations*
- *Mindful observation of thoughts without judgment*

- *Introduce relaxation exercises:*
- *Progressive muscle relaxation*
- *Guided imagery*
- *Simple yoga poses*

- *Encourage digital detox periods:*
- *Set aside device-free time daily*

- Plan occasional tech-free days or weekends

• Promote healthy sleep habits:
- Establish a digital curfew before bedtime
- Create a relaxing bedtime routine without screens

• Teach time management skills:
- Prioritize tasks and set realistic goals
- Use productivity apps to manage digital activities

• Foster real-world connections:
- Encourage face-to-face interactions with friends
- Promote participation in offline hobbies and activities

• Develop critical media literacy:
- Analyze and question online content
- Understand the curated nature of social media posts

• Practice gratitude:
- Keep a gratitude journal
- Share daily appreciation with family or friends

• Encourage physical activity:
- Regular exercise to reduce stress
- Outdoor activities to disconnect from the digital world

• *Teach positive self-talk:*
- *Challenge negative thoughts stemming from online experiences*
- *Develop self-affirmations*

• *Create a supportive environment:*
- *Open communication about digital pressures*
- *Validate feelings and experiences*

• *Introduce stress-relief activities:*
- *Art and creative expression*
- *Listening to calming music*
- *Engaging in nature-based activities*

• *Teach boundary-setting:*
- *How to say no to digital demands*
- *When and how to disconnect from online interactions*

• *Promote balanced self-image:*
- *Emphasize personal worth beyond online metrics*
- *Celebrate offline achievements and qualities*

By implementing these strategies, we can help children develop resilience against digital stress and anxiety, fostering a healthier relationship with technology.

Developing Emotional Resilience as a Goal

Helping youngsters develop coping strategies to deal with the challenges posed by digital technology is critical to building emotional resilience. Individuals' emotional resilience can be strengthened by encouraging open discussions about their experiences using online platforms and providing help when it is required. Here are critical

points for developing emotional resilience in children to cope with digital challenges:

• *Importance of emotional resilience:*
- *Helps children navigate online pressures and challenges*
- *Builds confidence in handling digital interactions*
- *Reduces vulnerability to cyberbullying and online stress*

• *Encourage open discussions:*
- *Create a safe space for children to share online experiences*
- *Listen without judgment to foster trust*
- *Validate their feelings and concerns*

• *Teach coping strategies:*
- *Mindfulness techniques for managing online stress*
- *Positive self-talk to counter negative online experiences*
- *Identifying trusted adults for support*

• *Develop critical thinking skills:*
- *Analyze online content and interactions objectively*
- *Recognize and challenge unrealistic social media standards*
- *Understand the impermanence of online trends*

• *Promote healthy online boundaries:*
- *Setting limits on social media use*
- *Learning to unfollow or mute negative influences*
- *Balancing online and offline relationships*

• *Build self-esteem independent of online validation:*
- *Encourage offline activities and achievements*
- *Reinforce self-worth beyond likes and followers*

• *Teach emotion regulation:*
- *Identifying and naming emotions triggered by online experiences*
- *Developing healthy outlets for strong emotions*

• *Foster digital empathy:*
- *Understanding the impact of online actions on others*
- *Encouraging kind and supportive online behaviour*

• *Provide ongoing support:*
- *Regular check-ins about online experiences*
- *Offering guidance on complex digital situations*

• *Collaborate with schools:*
- *Advocate for digital resilience education in curricula*
- *Participate in school-led digital wellness initiatives*

• Model resilient behavior:
- Demonstrate healthy coping strategies in your own digital life
- Show how to bounce back from online setbacks

Focusing on these aspects can help children build the emotional resilience to thrive in the digital world.

CHAPTER FIVE

Educational Strategies for Digital Wellbeing

Integrating Digital Wellbeing into Curriculum

Incorporating digital well-being education into the school curriculum can raise awareness and give students the tools to navigate the digital world responsibly. Lessons on digital citizenship, online ethics, and safe browsing practices can be included.

Teaching Mindful Technology Use

Mindful technology use involves knowing how, when, and why we use digital devices. Teaching children to be intentional with their screen time and to take regular breaks can foster healthier digital habits.

Here are key points on teaching mindful technology use to children:

• Define mindful technology use:
- Conscious awareness of how, when, and why we use devices
- Intentional engagement with digital content
- Balance between online and offline activities

• Teach self-awareness:
- Encourage children to notice their emotions during device use
- Help them recognize signs of digital fatigue or overuse

• Promote intentional screen time:
- Set clear purposes for device use (e.g., learning, communication, entertainment)
- Discourage mindless scrolling or channel surfing

• Implement regular digital breaks:
- Use techniques like the 20-20-20 rule for eye strain
- Encourage physical movement between screen

sessions

• *Foster critical thinking:*
- *Teach evaluation of online content's value and credibility*
- *Encourage questioning of time spent on various apps or sites*

• *Develop healthy digital habits:*
- *Create personalized guidelines for daily technology use*
- *Establish tech-free zones or times in the home*

• *Encourage mindful communication:*
- *Think before posting or sending messages*
- *Consider the impact of online words and actions*

• *Teach digital decluttering:*
- *Regularly review and remove unnecessary apps or subscriptions*
- *Organize digital spaces for efficiency and reduced stress*

• *Promote alternative activities:*
- *Encourage engagement in offline hobbies and interests*
- *Highlight the value of face-to-face interactions*

• Model mindful technology use:
- Demonstrate balanced and intentional device use as adults
- Discuss your strategies for mindful digital engagement

• Introduce mindfulness exercises:
- Practice short meditation or breathing exercises before device use
- Use mindfulness apps as tools for developing awareness

• Emphasize quality over quantity:
- Focus on the value derived from digital experiences
- Encourage selective and meaningful online interactions

By implementing these strategies, we can help children develop a more conscious and balanced approach to technology use, promote digital well-being, and foster healthier relationships with their devices.

Encouraging Critical Thinking Online

Developing critical thinking skills helps children discern credible information from misinformation online. Teaching them to evaluate sources, question content, and think critically about what they encounter online is essential.

• Importance of critical thinking online:
- Distinguishes credible information from misinformation
- Protects against manipulation and false narratives
- Enhances digital literacy and informed decision-making

• Key skills to teach:
- Source evaluation (credibility, authority, bias)
- Fact-checking techniques
- Recognizing logical fallacies and emotional manipulation

• Strategies for implementation:
- Encourage questioning of online content
- Practice analyzing news articles and social media posts
- Teach cross-referencing information with multiple sources

• Benefits:
- Develop informed digital citizens
- Improves overall cognitive abilities
- Enhances resilience against online threats and scams

- *Ongoing process:*
- *Regularly discuss online experiences*
- *Update skills as the digital landscape evolves*

CHAPTER SIX

Parental Guidance and Support

Defining Healthy Boundaries

Parents can significantly influence their children's digital behaviours. Setting healthy boundaries, such as limiting the time spent in front of a screen and establishing no-device zones (such as the dining table or bedroom), can help create a balanced digital environment within the home.

• Importance of parental influence:
- Parents are primary role models for digital

behaviour
- Children often mimic parents' technology habits
- Consistent guidance shapes long-term digital habits

• Setting time limits:
- Establish age-appropriate screen time guidelines
- Use parental control apps to enforce limits
- Gradually increase autonomy as children mature

• Creating no-device zones:
- Designate specific areas as tech-free (e.g., dining table, bedrooms)
- Encourage face-to-face interactions in these spaces
- Promote better sleep hygiene by keeping devices out of bedrooms

• Establishing device-free times:
- Implement tech-free hours (e.g., during meals, before bedtime)
- Create family time without digital distractions
- Encourage alternative activities during these periods

• *Leading by example:*
- *Parents should follow the same rules they set for children*
- *Demonstrate healthy technology use and work-life balance*
- *Show the value of offline activities and hobbies*

• *Open communication:*
- *Discuss the reasons behind digital boundaries*
- *Listen to children's perspectives and concerns*
- *Adjust rules collaboratively as needed*

• *Promoting alternative activities:*
- *Encourage outdoor play, reading, and creative pursuits*
- *Facilitate family activities that don't involve screens*
- *Support children's offline interests and hobbies*

• *Consistency and flexibility:*
- *Maintain consistent enforcement of boundaries*
- *Allow for occasional exceptions for exceptional circumstances*
- *Revisit and adjust boundaries as the family needs to change*

• *Positive reinforcement:*
- *Praise children for adhering to digital boundaries*
- *Highlight the benefits of balanced technology use*
- *Create rewards for meeting screen time goals*

• Educating about digital wellness:
- Explain the impact of excessive screen time on health
- Teach children to recognize signs of digital fatigue
- Encourage self-regulation as they grow older

By implementing these strategies, parents can create a home environment that fosters healthy digital habits and overall well-being for their children.

Monitoring and reducing the amount of usage

Monitoring youngsters' digital activities and exercising moderation over their Internet use is necessary. Parental control software can assist in managing screen time and restricting access to unsuitable content.

• Importance of parental influence:
- Parents are primary role models for digital behaviour

- Children often mimic parents' technology habits
- Consistent guidance shapes long-term digital habits

• Setting time limits:
- Establish age-appropriate screen time guidelines
- Use parental control apps to enforce limits
- Gradually increase autonomy as children mature

• Creating no-device zones:
- Designate specific areas as tech-free (e.g., dining table, bedrooms)
- Encourage face-to-face interactions in these spaces
- Promote better sleep hygiene by keeping devices out of bedrooms

• Establishing device-free times:
- Implement tech-free hours (e.g., during meals, before bedtime)
- Create family time without digital distractions
- Encourage alternative activities during these periods

• Leading by example:
- Parents should follow the same rules they set for children
- Demonstrate healthy technology use and work-life balance
- Show the value of offline activities and hobbies

• *Open communication:*
- *Discuss the reasons behind digital boundaries*
- *Listen to children's perspectives and concerns*
- *Adjust rules collaboratively as needed*

• *Promoting alternative activities:*
- *Encourage outdoor play, reading, and creative pursuits*
- *Facilitate family activities that don't involve screens*
- *Support children's offline interests and hobbies*

• *Consistency and flexibility:*
- *Maintain consistent enforcement of boundaries*
- *Allow for occasional exceptions for exceptional circumstances*
- *Revisit and adjust boundaries as the family needs to change*

• *Positive reinforcement:*
- *Praise children for adhering to digital boundaries*
- *Highlight the benefits of balanced technology use*
- *Create rewards for meeting screen time goals*

• *Educating about digital wellness:*
- *Explain the impact of excessive screen time on health*
- *Teach children to recognize signs of digital fatigue*
- *Encourage self-regulation as they grow older*

By implementing these strategies, parents can create a home environment that fosters healthy digital habits and overall well-being for their children.

Open Communication Regarding Experiences Obtained Online

Children are more likely to feel supported when encouraged to communicate openly about their experiences online. Having a conversation about the positive and negative aspects of their internet connections can potentially provide significant insights and help.

-

Fostering Trust: Open communication between children and parents creates a safe space for youngsters to share their internet experiences without fear of judgment or punishment.

-

Cyberbullying, improper content, and stranger contact can be identified by encouraging youngsters to communicate about their online encounters. Early detection allows prompt treatment.

-

Conversations about online activity give parents insight into digital trends and the platforms and materials their children are using. With this knowledge, parents can better guide their children.

-

Promoting Positive utilize: Discussing the internet's educational and creative resources helps youngsters to use it properly.

-

Building Critical Thinking: Open discourse helps kids think critically about online interactions. They learn to doubt information and value digital citizenship.

- *The cyberbullying discussion provides emotional support and reassurance. Validated children are more inclined to ask for aid.*

- *Boundaries: Open communication between parents and children helps set appropriate limits and screen time limitations for a balanced digital existence.*

CHAPTER SEVEN

Creating a Supportive School Environment

Policies for Digital Wellbeing

Establishing school policies that promote digital well-being can create a supportive environment. These policies might include guidelines for screen time, digital etiquette, and online safety.

Here are key points for establishing school policies for digital well-being:

• *Develop comprehensive digital well-being policies:*
- *Involve administrators, teachers, parents, and students in policy creation*
- *Align with broader educational and health objectives*

• *Set clear screen time guidelines:*
- *Define appropriate device usage during school hours*
- *Establish limits for homework and after-school activities*

• *Implement digital etiquette rules:*
- *Create a code of conduct for online interactions*
- *Address cyberbullying and appropriate social media use*

• *Prioritize online safety:*
- *Establish protocols for safe internet use in school*
- *Educate on privacy settings and data protection*

• *Integrate digital literacy into the curriculum:*
- *Teach critical thinking skills for evaluating online content*
- *Include lessons on recognizing and avoiding online risks*

• *Promote balanced technology use:*
- *Encourage tech-free zones or times during the school day*

- *Support a mix of digital and traditional learning methods*

• *Address physical health concerns:*
- *Implement ergonomic guidelines for device use*
- *Encourage regular breaks and physical activity*

• *Support mental health:*
- *Provide resources for managing digital stress and anxiety*
- *Offer counseling for technology-related issues*

• *Foster positive digital citizenship:*
- *Teach responsible and ethical online behaviour*
- *Encourage positive contributions to online communities*

• *Implement monitoring and filtering systems:*
- *Use appropriate software to ensure safe browsing at school*
- *Respect student privacy while maintaining safety*

• *Provide teacher training:*
- *Equip educators with skills to model and teach digital well-being*
- *Keep staff updated on emerging digital trends and challenges*

• *Engage parents:*
- *Communicate school policies to families*
- *Offer resources for supporting digital well-being at home*

• *Regular policy review:*
- *Update guidelines to address the evolving technology landscape*
- *Seek feedback from all stakeholders for continuous improvement*

• *Create accountability measures:*
- *Establish consequences for policy violations*
- *Recognize and reward positive digital behaviours*

By implementing these policies, schools can create a supportive environment that promotes digital well-being and prepares students for responsible technology use in their future lives.

Training for Teachers and Staff

Providing teachers and staff with training on digital well-being can equip them with the knowledge and skills to support students. This training can cover topics like recognizing signs of digital addiction, managing cyberbullying, and promoting healthy digital habits. Digital well-being is a critical aspect of modern education that requires a comprehensive and proactive approach. By providing thorough training for teachers and staff, schools can create a supportive environment

that addresses the complex challenges of the digital age.

This training empowers educators to recognize and address issues like digital addiction and cyberbullying, which can significantly impact students' mental health and academic performance. It also equips them with strategies to promote healthy digital habits, ensuring that technology enhances rather than detracts from the learning experience.

Building a Culture of Digital Responsibility

Creating a culture of digital responsibility involves promoting awareness and accountability among students. Encouraging responsible digital behaviour and recognizing positive digital habits can foster a healthy digital culture. The widespread use of technology in classrooms and everyday life has numerous problems, but one all-encompassing answer is to promote a culture of digital responsibility. This strategy reaches the heart of digital wellness problems by encouraging a shared

dedication to ethical tech use.

- *Making sure everyone in the school community knows what it means to be a responsible digital citizen is the first step in finding a solution to the problem of digital responsibility. In this sense, being tech-savvy is being mindful of one's digital imprint, using the internet responsibly and ethically, and consuming technology in moderation.*

- *One crucial part of this answer is raising awareness. The school is up-to-date on the latest IT news and developments thanks to frequent meetings, seminars, and student-run projects. This continuous education helps everyone keep up with the ever-changing digital scene.*

- *Responsibility also plays a crucial role. The school builds a foundation for responsible digital activity by setting clear rules for online conduct and consistent punishments for misbehaviour. Because they encourage students to be active participants in managing their own digital space, peer accountability programs have the potential to be highly effective.*

- *Rules and punishments are not the only way to promote responsible behaviour online. The program encourages students to think critically about their digital interactions, incorporates digital citizenship into the curriculum, and allows them to practice good online habits. By taking the initiative, we can ensure that our pupils learn to navigate the internet responsibly.*

- *Recognizing and rewarding strong digital habits encourages pupils to continue these activities and promotes good conduct. Awards, displays, and positive reinforcement can foster a culture that values and celebrates ethical digital use.*

- *Establishing a supportive atmosphere is crucial for this culture to flourish. Students are more likely to feel comfortable discussing and resolving digital concerns when there is an open conversation about them, safe reporting channels for online difficulties, and mentorship programs.*

- *By involving the larger community, such as parents and local businesses, the culture of digital responsibility can be expanded beyond the confines of schools. By covering all bases, we can ensure that kids hear the same lessons about being responsible with technology in all parts of their lives.*

- *Fostering student-led initiatives and collaborative projects in schools can set an excellent example for the responsible and constructive use of technology. This practical experience is crucial for students to grasp digital technology's possibilities and obligations fully.*

•

Lastly, these initiatives should be continuously evaluated and adjusted so that the culture of digital responsibility can keep up with ever-changing technology. Schools' ability to tackle new digital difficulties as they arise makes maintaining a solid and adaptable digital wellness program possible.

CHAPTER EIGHT

Technological Tools for Digital Wellbeing

Apps and Tools for Managing Screen Time

Numerous apps and tools can help manage screen time and promote digital well-being.

Google offers:

https://experiments.withgoogle.com/collection/ digitalwellbeing

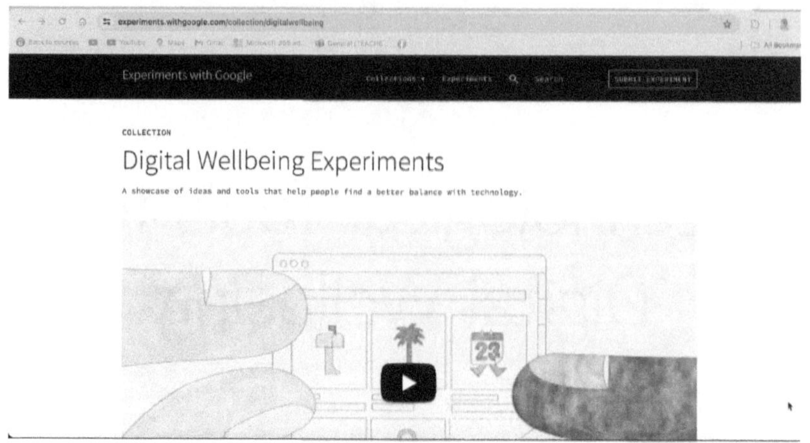

https://experiments.withgoogle.com/collection/
digitalwellbeing

1. Emotion Recognition

Machine learning helps platforms like Affectiva recognize human emotions and expressions. Before hitting the wall, emotion recognition can track mood swings or burnout, indicating the need for self-care or intervention.

Media and advertising marketers can use the human perception AI software to monitor facial and vocal emotions to evaluate media content's emotional impact.

2. EAPs with AI

Artificial intelligence-driven Employee Assistance Programs (EAPs) are improving employee mental health. EAPs can become more effective as AI technology advances.

On Ginger.io, you can get on-demand virtual help that uses behavioural insights and machine learning to detect symptoms, connect you with doctors, and improve mental health.

3. Personal Digital Coaches

With more intelligent and human-like tailored digital coaches, the focus will change from support to real-time contact with employees to boost motivation, productivity, and stress.

Woebot and Wysa are pioneering conversational chatbots that use Cognitive Behavioral Therapy (CBT) to improve mental health and self-awareness.

4. Adv. Analytics

Advanced analytics can illuminate personal and corporate productivity. Clockwise and Worklytics use machine learning algorithms to analyze meeting and collaboration patterns to optimize calls and avoid productivity issues.

Time and resource efficiency can depend on these insights.

5. Predictive Tasking

AI can make task management systems more intuitive and efficient. Based on previous data and user behaviour, Todoist and TimeHero schedule, prioritize and set deadlines.

The above tools can set usage limits, track screen time, and provide reminders to take breaks.

• *Purpose of screen time management tools:*
- *Help users monitor and control device usage*
- *Promote healthier digital habits*
- *Support overall digital well-being*

• *Types of apps and tools available:*
- *Built-in operating system features (e.g., Screen Time for iOS, Digital Wellbeing for Android)*
- *Third-party applications for various platforms*
- *Browser extensions for computer use*

• *Key features of these tools:*
- *Screen time tracking and reporting*
- *App usage breakdown*
- *Time limit setting for specific apps or categories*
- *Scheduled downtime periods*
- *Reminders for breaks or device-free time*
- *Content filtering and app-blocking options*

• *Benefits of using these tools:*
- *Increased awareness of digital habits*
- *Support for self-regulation and discipline*
- *Reduction in mindless scrolling and app usage*
- *Promotion of balanced technology use*

- Improved focus and productivity

• Considerations when choosing tools:
- Age-appropriateness for children
- Cross-platform compatibility
- Customization options
- Privacy and data security features
- Ease of use and user interface

• Implementation strategies:
- Gradual introduction to avoid resistance
- Family discussions on tool selection and usage rules
- Regular review and adjustment of settings
- Combining tool use with broader digital wellness education

• Limitations to keep in mind:
- Not a substitute for self-discipline and education
- Possibility of workarounds, especially for tech-savvy users
- Need for consistent enforcement and monitoring

Resources for Online Safety

Resources that educate children about online safety can empower them to navigate the digital world securely. These resources might include interactive games, educational videos, and informative websites.

• *Types of online safety resources:*
- *Interactive educational games*
- *Animated videos and short films*
- *Informative websites and blogs*
- *E-learning modules and courses*
- *Downloadable guides and worksheets*
- *Podcasts and audio resources*
- *Social media campaigns and challenges*

• *Key topics covered:*
- *Protecting personal information*
- *Recognizing and avoiding online scams*
- *Cyberbullying awareness and prevention*
- *Safe social media practices*
- *Understanding digital footprints*
- *Identifying fake news and misinformation*
- *Secure password management*
- *Safe online gaming*

• *Benefits of these resources:*
- *Age-appropriate content for different learning stages*
- *Engaging formats that appeal to children and teens*
- *Interactive elements for hands-on learning*
- *Regular updates to address emerging online*

threats
- Accessibility from various devices and platforms

• Implementation strategies:
- Integration into school curricula
- Parent-child joint learning sessions
- Regular "online safety" days or weeks
- Peer-to-peer teaching initiatives
- Gamification of online safety lessons

• Notable organizations providing resources:
- National cybersecurity agencies
- Non-profit internet safety organizations
- Tech companies' digital literacy programs
- Educational institutions and universities

• Customization and localization:
- Resources tailored to specific age groups
- Content adapted for different cultural contexts
- Materials available in multiple languages

• Evaluation and effectiveness:
- Regular assessment of resource impact
- Feedback mechanisms for continuous improvement
- Long-term studies on behavioural changes

Platforms for Mental Health Support

Digital platforms offering mental health support can provide valuable resources for children. These platforms might include counselling services, mental health apps, and online support groups.

• Types of digital mental health platforms:
- Online counselling services
- Mental health apps for mood tracking and self-help
- Virtual support groups and forums
- AI-powered chatbots for immediate support
- Teletherapy platforms connecting users with professionals

• Key features:
- Anonymity options for user comfort
- 24/7 accessibility
- Interactive tools for stress management and mindfulness
- Educational resources on mental health topics
- Crisis helpline integration

• Benefits:
- Reduced stigma around seeking help
- Increased access to support, especially in remote areas
- Early intervention possibilities
- Customized support based on individual needs
- Complementary to traditional therapy

• Considerations:

- Ensuring age-appropriate content and interactions

- Maintaining user privacy and data security

- Professional oversight and moderation

CHAPTER NINE

Emerging Technologies & Digital Wellbeing

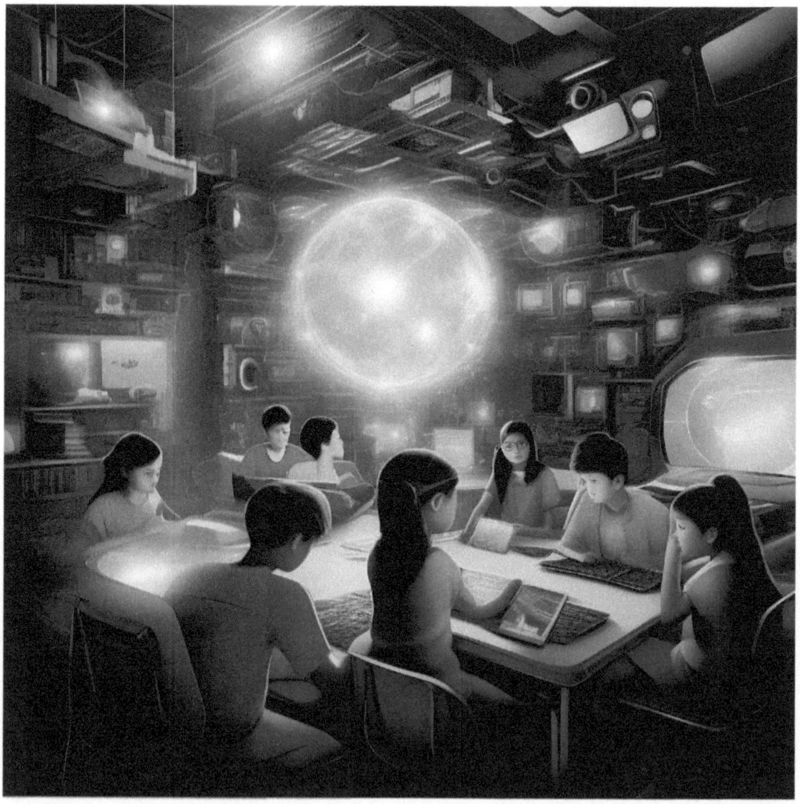

Exploring emerging technologies that can impact digital well-being is essential for staying ahead of the curve. This might include advancements in artificial intelligence, virtual reality, and wearable technology.

- *Artificial Intelligence (AI) is rapidly evolving, offering potential benefits and risks for digital well-being. AI-powered tools could provide personalized recommendations for healthy digital habits, but they also raise concerns about data privacy and algorithmic bias. It's essential to develop AI systems that prioritize user well-being and transparency.*

- *Virtual Reality (VR) and Augmented Reality (AR) technologies are expanding beyond gaming, entering educational and social spaces. While they offer immersive learning experiences and new forms of social interaction, they also present risks of addiction and detachment from the physical world. Developing guidelines for healthy VR/AR use will be crucial.*

- *Wearable technology is becoming increasingly sophisticated, with devices capable of monitoring various physical and mental health aspects. These devices could provide valuable data for managing digital well-being, but they also raise questions about constant health surveillance and data security.*

-

The Internet of Things (IoT) is creating more connected environments, which could streamline daily tasks but also lead to increased screen time and tech dependency. Balancing convenience with mindful tech use will be a crucial challenge.

Though still in the early stages, brain-computer interfaces could revolutionize how we interact with technology. While they promise enhanced accessibility and efficiency, they also raise profound questions about cognitive autonomy and mental privacy.

As these technologies evolve, it's crucial to:
1. Conduct ongoing research on their impact on wellbeing
2. Develop adaptive policies and guidelines
3. Educate users about responsible use
4. Encourage ethical development that prioritizes user wellbeing
5. Foster interdisciplinary collaboration to address complex challenges

Staying informed and proactive about these emerging technologies will be vital in promoting digital well-being in an increasingly tech-driven future.

The Evolving Digital Landscape

Understanding the evolving digital landscape helps anticipate future challenges and opportunities. Staying informed about trends and changes in digital technology is crucial for promoting digital well-being.

The digital landscape is constantly changing, with new technologies, platforms, and trends emerging at a rapid pace. This dynamic environment presents opportunities and challenges for digital well-being.

Social media platforms continue to evolve, introducing features that can either enhance or potentially harm user well-being. For instance, the rise of short-form video content platforms has changed how information is consumed, potentially impacting attention spans and information retention.

The increasing prevalence of AI and machine learning in everyday applications reshapes user experiences. While these technologies can offer personalized experiences, they raise concerns about data privacy and algorithmic bias.

The shift towards remote work and online education, accelerated by global events, has blurred the lines between personal and professional digital spaces. This trend necessitates new approaches to maintaining work-life balance and managing screen time.

Emerging technologies like virtual and augmented reality create more immersive digital experiences, which may profoundly affect social interactions and cognitive processes.

The growing awareness of digital well-being influences technology design, with more companies incorporating well-being features into their products.

To effectively promote digital well-being in this evolving landscape:

1. Stay informed about emerging technologies and trends
2. Critically evaluate the potential impacts of new digital tools
3. Adapt digital wellbeing strategies to address new challenges
4. Encourage ongoing research into the effects of new technologies

5. *Foster digital literacy to help users navigate the changing landscape*

By remaining vigilant and adaptable, we can better prepare for future digital well-being challenges and harness technological advancements' positive potential.

Preparing for the Future

Preparing for the future involves equipping children with the skills and knowledge to navigate the digital world confidently. Fostering adaptability, resilience, and critical thinking will help them thrive in an ever-changing digital environment.

Preparing children for the future digital landscape is crucial. Key strategies include:

- *Developing digital literacy skills*

- *Fostering critical thinking abilities*

- *Encouraging adaptability to new technologies*

- *Building emotional resilience for online challenges*

- *Teaching responsible digital citizenship*

- *Promoting a growth mindset towards technology*

-

Balancing tech skills with human-centric abilities

- *Emphasizing ethical decision-making in digital spaces*

- *Cultivating creativity by using digital tools*

- *Encouraging continuous learning about emerging tech*

By focusing on these areas, we equip children with a robust toolkit to navigate the evolving digital world. This preparation goes beyond mere technical skills, encompassing the cognitive, emotional, and ethical competencies needed to thrive in a technology-driven future. The goal is to create confident, responsible, and innovative digital citizens.

CHAPTER TEN

100 Ways Towards Digital Wellness

1.

Use digital financial management tools

2.

Online, practice digital empathy.

3.

Create a digital photo management system.

4.

Reduce screen time with voice assistants.

5.

Use mobile device ergonomics.

6.

Use digital meal planners and grocery lists.

7.

Set up digital receipt management.

8.

Digital instruments for language learning

9.

Be wary when reading online news.

10.

Digital time zone management tools

11.

Set up digital warranty management.

12.

Digital tools for virtual workouts

13.

Use video conferencing etiquette.

14.

Track your mood digitally.

15.

A digital health record management system

16.

Practice mindful breathing with technology.

17.

Declutter your digital life periodically.

18.

Digitally create and share to-do lists.

19.

Manage digital contacts with a system.

20.

Journal digitally.

21.

Shop online safely.

22.

Use digital meditation timers.

23.

Set up digital music library management.

24.

Digitally track water intake.

25.

Avoid bad posture during long gaming sessions.

26.

Digitally track screen time.

27.

Set up digital book library management.

28.

Digital technologies enable collaborative brainstorming.

29.

Be wary of location services.

30.

Track personal carbon footprint digitally.

31.

Create a digital art collection management system.

32.

Digital technologies help create good habits.

33.

Responsible for online sharing of personal data

34.

Digitally track device battery health.

35.

Systematize digital recipe management.

36.

Digitally create and share family photo albums.

37.

Mindful social media messaging

38.

Digital technologies track and improve typing speed.

39.

Create a digital academic resource management system.

40.

Create and manage appreciation lists digitally.

41.

Cloud storage allows cross-device access.

42.

Learn to spot and avoid online scams

43.

Be digitally responsible.

44.

Using noise-cancelling headphones for focus

45.

Use digital filing.

46.

Apps for guided meditation or mindfulness

47.

Regularly clean and maintain devices

48.

Physical alarm clocks instead of phones

49.

Technology multitasking should be limited.

50.

Learn digital literacy

51.

Control kids' devices with parental controls.

52.

Keep passwords clean.

53.

VPNs protect online privacy.

54.

Create a "digital sunset" before bed.

55.

For efficiency, use text expansion tools.

56.

Clear browser cache and cookies regularly.

57.

Use ad-blockers for a cleaner surfing experience and maintain appropriate posture when using devices.

58.

Organize with digital note-taking applications.

59.

Personal improvement through online learning

60.

Time-tracking apps boost productivity.

61.

Use email management tactics.

62.

Track habits digitally.

63.

Post mindfully on social media.

64.

Screen sharing aids collaboration.

65.

Set up digital document signature.

66.

Protect Wi-Fi networks with passwords.

67.

Behave well on webcam.

68.

Set and track goals digitally.

69.

Set up digital subscription management.

70.

Be cautious when browsing.

71.

Use password managers for safety.

72.

Frequently change privacy settings.

73.

Master keyboard shortcuts for efficiency.

74.

Reduce typing with voice-to-text.

75.

Regularly organize digital files.

76.

Stop receiving unwanted emails.

77.

Use two-factor authentication.

78.

Computer work at a standing desk

79.

Take regular stretching breaks.

80.

Device ergonomics should be learned.

81.

Track and enhance sleep with apps.

82.

Be vigilant in online communities.

83.

Limit work-related digital communication.

84.

Digital calendars improve time management.

85.

Be digitally minimalist.

86.

Create a positive social media feed.

87.

Block websites at work.

88.

Use "touch it once" for emails.

89.

Back up essential data regularly.

90.

Limit screen time

91.

Filter blue light.

92.

Use 20-20-20 for eye strain.

93.

Disable unnecessary alerts

94.

Block unfavourable social media accounts

95.

Make tech-free zones at home.

96.

Schedule digital detox days.

97.

Use productivity applications to focus.

98.

Implement "no phones at meals."

99. *Devices out of the bedroom*

100. *Practice empathy online*

About The Author

Dheeraj Mehrotra, MS, MPhil, PhD (Education Management)., a white and a yellow belt in SIX SIGMA, a Certified NLP Business Diploma holder, is an Educational Innovator, Author, with expertise in Six Sigma In Education, Academic Audits, Neuro-Linguistic Programming (NLP), Total Quality Management In Education, an Experiential Educator, a CBSE Resource towards School Assessment (SQAA), CCE, JIT, Five S, and KAIZEN. He has authored over 100 books on computer science, AI, digital body language, NLP, quality circles, school management, classroom effectiveness, and safety and security. A former Principal at De Indian Public School, New Delhi, (INDIA), NPS International School, Guwahati, and Education Officer at GEMS, Gurgaon, with ample teaching experience of over Three Decades, he is a certified Trainer for Quality Circles/ TQM in Education and QCI Standards for School Accreditation/ School Audits and Management. He has also been honoured with the President of India's National Teacher Award in 2006 and the Best Science Teacher State Award (By the Ministry of Science and Technology, State of UP), Innovation in Education for his inception of Six Sigma In Education by Education Watch, New Delhi and Education World- Best Teacher Award, BOLT Learner Teacher Award by Air India, 'Innovation in Education Award 2016' by Higher Education Forum (HEF), Gujarat Chapter, among others. He has developed over 150 FREE EDUCATIONAL MOBILE Apps for the Google Play Store exclusively for Teachers, Students, and Parents. This work has been recognised by the LIMCA BOOK OF RECORDS and INDIA BOOK OF RECORDS as the only Indian to draw that feast. As a founder president of the IoT Society of India, he also promotes Technology Globally. Dr Mehrotra is presently engaged as a PRINCIPAL at KUNWARS GLOBAL SCHOOL, Lucknow, India. He has conducted over 2000 workshops globally on "Excellence In Education" integrated with Total Quality Management and Six

Sigma, Technology Integration in Education (TIE), Developing towards being ROCKSTAR TEACHERS, including Cyberspace, Cyber Security, Classroom Management, School Leadership & Management, and Innovative teaching within classrooms via Mind Maps, NLP and Experiential Learning in Academics. He is an active TEDx speaker and can be viewed on the YouTube TEDx channel. As a premium UDEMY Instructor, he has developed over 500 courses and caters to over 8 Lakh students from 180 countries. He can be visited at www.authordheerajmehrotra.com

https://www.udemy.com/user/dr-dheeraj-mehrotra/

Books By The Same Author

Books

Cyber Security
For Kids
2022

Classroom
Teaching Ideas
2022

BASICS OF
ARTIFICIAL...
2019

Smart Career
Planner
2020

Student
Engagement...
2022

Marketing
Mantras For...
2021

Tools And Tips
For Teaching...
2021

Quality Circles
in Schools
2022

Basics of
Artificial...
2021

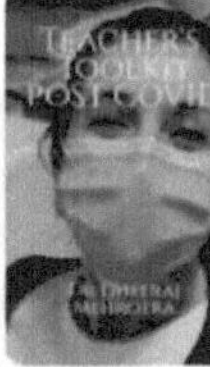

Teacher's
Toolkit Post...
2021

AI Basics for
School...
2019

Basics of Go
Programming
2022

www.authordheerajmehrotra.com

Optimising Educational...

2022

High Performance...

2020

Learning Beyond COVID

2022

Secrets to Raising a...

2022

101 SCHOOL MANAGEME...

2017

Digital Body Language

2020

The Quality Icon

2022

Academic Quality...

2022

The One Minute Educator

2021

Digital Wellbeing For...

2022

The 64 Kalas of Krishna For...

2023

Risk Management...

2022

www.authordheerajmehrotra.com

R Programming For Beginners
2021

Impact of Information...
2021

Pedagogical Practices to...
2022

Motivating & Quality...
2022

Child Safeguarding ...
2022

Climate Classroom
2021

NEP 2020- At a Glance for...
2021

Street Smart Teaching...
2021

Optimal Child Development
2022

Roadmap To A New Normal...
2020

Teaching in a Digital Age
2022

Conscious Parenting
2021

School

Disruptive

Ways to

100 Ideas For

100 Green

Academic

www.authordheerajmehrotra.com

www.ingramcontent.com/pod-product-compliance
Lightning Source LLC
Chambersburg PA
CBHW031305130726
47988CB00007B/2731